Body & Glass

Wave Books

Seattle/New York

Body & Glass   Rodney Koeneke

Published by Wave Books

www.wavepoetry.com

Copyright © 2018 by Rodney Koeneke

All rights reserved

Wave Books titles are distributed to the trade by

Consortium Book Sales and Distribution

Phone: 800-283-3572 / SAN 631-760X

Library of Congress Cataloging-in-Publication Data

Names: Koeneke, Rodney, author.

Title: Body & glass / Rodney Koeneke.

Other titles: Poems. Selection | Body and glass

Description: First Edition. | Seattle : Wave Books, [2018]

Identifiers: LCCN 2017033944 | ISBN 9781940696676

   (limited edition hardcover) | ISBN 9781940696683 (trade pbk.)

Classification: LCC PS3611.O363 A6 2018 | DDC 811/.6—dc23

LC record available at https://lccn.loc.gov/2017033944

Designed by Quemadura

Printed in the United States of America

9 8 7 6 5 4 3 2 1

First Edition

Wave Books 071

for Lesley   *immer noch*

And for what reason make anything that is not for flight?

—Stephen Rodefer

Body & Glass

his armored team

Through the ribbed hall I move continually
with my armored team, my

          armored team

exuberant satellites:

       fall anywhere,

            break anything.

tarnish the coppice, punk autumn

Tarnish the coppice, punk autumn
kick smug green down from trees.
Kings die like we die, kings
are just bumps on furzed glebes.
See how the fallen enjoy
being beaten, look at the bishop
sit there and twist his gemmed rings.

Desert fathers hector Caesars
burning on their stamp-sized emperies.
Cumuli deploy, dissolve, courtiers
egressing from a room. Duende
thrums in the crevices of festivals

While we play statistics
in the episteme's census,
amours and their errors on
charts in fresh colors: russet,
umber, cobalt, verdigris.

song of the south

Ponies nicker in paddocks,
cows consider ruefully
inedible carpets of flowers.

Dressed in good silks,
I stayed loyal to my lord
and so stained them.

There were orchestras
and opulence but times,
as the world, will change.

The garden's colored
globes of light depend
on the hiddenest filaments.

As geese think to migrate,
at last I come to understand
my context—the coaches

I waved from rattled with decorous
plangency. What was it
while in them I missed?

thanks to the 250+ participants

Because the mirror is broken on your Prius
I have come to believe more firmly
In the purpose of your conference—
A need to explain the broken
To the broken, a feeling of being uneasy
Looking backward at destruction,
Boom dropped through the frame
Of tableau after gold tableau.
I'm not so afraid of hands
Not getting dirty, the humus
Being rotored in an academic field,
But your dark hair in its surplus
Through the bent glass on the Prius—
I choose this to remember from my visit
To the conference: the thingness
Of things yoked in shared obsolescence,
Structure of you moving
While structure itself never moves.

psalmish

Spring romps drunk
in Monday clothes
but leaves no space for crying

Where we would have business
of woofing and wefting
till I forget
what poem is again

Because I once loved you
who taught me connection
scholar of buckles
solderer's song

Weaver and woven
each broken in season

From antiphons' slurring
surmising the psalm

scott walker sings

Rains have arrived,
filling a ripped canopy with the building's
spoiled water. What would it take
for the month to invest us
with everyone's regular happiness
reliably discovered under evening's
growing clutter, pulled upward on wires
to access and confound the ordinary
properties of intermission?

Pumps fill swales till green
has place to rest in, alone in the lane
crossed by wet rocks
where age gets stuck and counts
itself as nothing, is sick
of the mood of being old,
of cold things meter brings you:
drops beat loose slates,
froth swells drain's loud pan.

syrtos

The stock's eye shut and it yawned.
Always their tranche is used badly—their dove

Is a creature with little of the love.
What they and their ken can cadge

From the bower, they cadge. But I
And my foot will make them work,

Stamp to upset the spirit lamp
Whose flames unpeeled our ceilings

Singeing life in open rooms
Where greenness ought to wander

Blackened a little, but not unloved.
You go: unhook the latch

And call the lift. Although you have held
Up a household, it's nice

To simply leave now, alone in the green
That becomes you, that is awesome.

The thinkers who think
Have expended much energy—

At long last, just the *opa*

the new hellenism

This poem depicts him in a railway
which is an emotion, a vessel for temporal
transit and decay. It's a very sad poem,
urging how already for Greeks
Death and Sleep were twins:
sunning in temples, losing
the day's meter—life
so surprising in its healing
and changing that way.

Its power then traded
for numbers of people: Zoe
dragging digits through the absinthe,
Bios swelling forests into rings. Calendars,
like Keats, belong to dying—that, too,
is an emotion, superimposed upon characters
slid far below the melancholic fashion,
collapsing at the station with a ticket
folded crisply in a clutch.

The brainiest in Greece were frankly tragic.
Inspired the people, yet civilized
sadness: nothing to an empery but trauma

stretched to take in larger things.
The world belongs to beauty, what
corrupts it—a raw new way
to journey through emotion,
winners whose humility has failed.

This then becomes a question
to see if you are human: have
beauty but too young to fully
use it? Or age in ancient industries
consumed with wasted stumps?

to an indie friend in havasu

They do not want you any closer here.
Of the few who will need you to administrate the ruins
Most stand behind their desks and are pure business.
The sky, their sky, an escalation of lake
Shifts blue from duct to dam to tap
While inside you try to relax with your images

As if in a smoky haze down a graded incline
From the mountains where your style,
Upper item on the invoice, is a charging
For your coming as the obverse of their dream.

Film sitting in a camera, film is dead
Though light still drops its Roman coins
For Roman kids to find. Because
The body's greeds have come to bore you—
Long books on being happy and alive—
The sun, whose broad estate neglects the bookish,
It hasn't left you even one *centime*.

whose voice to have called you

Whose voice to have called you
And brought you to breathing
So mute as you tarry,
Enclosed in career?

Whose thoughts aren't like your thoughts
But strips of bright
Silver, bringing you constants
On dead twisting paths

Till words couldn't keep you
Collected in hours
Advanced in a body
Confused with the grass

To show us by falling
More reasons for leaving
Thought's office to leave you
In sleep without fear

humber, severn, mersey, thames, and ouse

Which fish toss in the Humber?
What thanes control the sluice?
Wherever Thames has said its name
It says it loud and lordly. The Mersey
Bears its mess of ships that slide
From oily docks, Clyde turns giant
Dynamos, subtle Severn stutters code
No lovers ever con. Companionable
Avon picks up readers, Great Stour loses them
In clever strings of artificial lakes. Drains
Supplement the Medway, weirs that used
To slow the Ouse now dry above the catchments.
Turn a knob, the Leven groans; foam
From the chemical Wandle wends to warm
The sea. Shrunk bergs—disappearing
Aristocracies—eat banks and waste
The chanceries, swamp towns,
Wreck lots, top cars, sink roofs, free
Humber, Severn, Mersey,
Thames, and Ouse.

an epitaph on the french prophets

Always they have decided to be more ready
Pausing to regard us from the summits where they are
Crowns cooled in ashes, vacated palaces
Movement through the passages that should have led to light

Where first they had convened to be more like us—
Bloody placards twisting from a pole
A parliament of doubters ratified by simple waiting
Like doubt had been the latest kind of friend

Who sat with us to keep the common measure
No faction telling Sion what a mountain ought to mean
No need for muddy captains, captains' need to lead us further
Creatures tired being foreign, pushing out to distant homes

To find a kinder sovereign, occulted like a father
Content to promise, dapple, dribble, gild—stooped hero
Speaking closely, a common man of business: "I'm calling
You," he's saying, "but you keep not hearing me."

young historian's scoring rubric

It's why we have dope—to blaze
then nod on a scale whose pain
is my thesis forgot in a mesh
of working parts. Free sirens
till they're hooked by fellahin,

Agree to record them, dye them
cerulean, rewriting their papers
in excellent grammar—they paid
for those papers, paper cites directly
from chants one once directed at the Sun.

Analysis is solid, and done
in a historical way, but free
from all history—balloon on
a tether with girl in a picture
primary evidence let fly away.

berceuse

Adherent of storms
and untimely
weather, how you
sleep where ashes
are blowing. I bring
my small light
that kids use
for comfort, pull up
the ratty quilts until
what isn't closer doesn't
matter—night the executrix
appoints, deletes
patricians telling
children Rome
is burning but is
that right, blue
satellite?

his first time in ankara

the embassies of Ankara are always at a standstill
—George Seferis, *Days of 1945–1951*

For the first time in Ankara, sparrow
move down to me as evening starts to slow
and inside my hotel room
we'll take up with Cavafy here again—
days in broken bottles, days
of 1910. I pass doubts

In my tracksuit, proceed through friends
who help me with my outfits, friends
who know the outfits show the love.
You cannot wait for times
of fame, but finish one
good strophe and the art
has been complete.

I trample over carpets
embroidered for the courtyard—
all rites invite a violence, release
a tragedy. Let minarets apologize
or minsters or gold domes: we
will not speak in content's

tenements, a sparrow
who flies and is cheerful
is a poem for all people,
a form to lift the district,
the district's formal friend.

Erinyes, rest. You'll have
new things to rend in time,
whole Smyrnas ashed in urns.
The embassies of Ankara are always
at a standstill; traveler, build
your nervous perch
on this hotel's disused edge.

he accounts for the art's current state

Either in spirit a mocking renewal
or attempts to replace the Alps
they make no sense
unless you should turn to avoid them
beside the tiny grains of intuition
squabbling there over who dropped them,
taught them to grow on the shrines.

Once dreams stop, then the coitus
it's best to be polemic—
sun is sense is field is form
and after, all gets splendid.

another hapless functionary

Another hapless functionary
placed to block the show.
Love made like a lectionary:
chapter, snippet, curse.
Troubles shorten February,
iced bulbs hoard up woes
colorless as conscience,
but loved for that no worse.
It's all we could demand now:
green earth under snow.

schottische

You are old but
if possible I'd
   like to keep

Moving, filling
the meter step
   after step we

Cruise foreign
cities, immanence
   burning up woods

In a winter, steed
and a lance and
   Plantagenet weather

Tangle of prints
involving the tower
   you still won't

Believe in my
sovereign my error to
   punk and to ruin I

Follow you moving
because of the
  season to which we're

Returning adjusted
in status to wander
  on commons

So simple so
long just to
  enter that ground.

**first there's his heart
destroying the strega**

First there's my heart
destroying the Strega
then come the roses
that float in the bath

Come to the feast
I set for you, heart
leave your long crunch
in the upstate leaves

A crown of forgetting
shedding its petals
tear out the petals
forgive the long debt

For simple new fashions
the kids are exchanging
until they have turned
in the same small space

To find that the heart
is wanton and wanders
but where will it wander
to wear its new crown

Petals are pulled
and after regretted
now finish the Strega
come cool in the bath.

passerine

What is there in that other
world is there as flat black
silhouettes of great-spanned
birds on breezeway glass so
passerines, thick protestants
ferocious in their inwardness
don't drowse a beat before the
god glass they can't see strikes
down in Darwin's wonted curve
but swerve, survive in debt to
simple human threat—hope's
negative, a love reversed—till
night arrive to deepen light,
depth dies to suffer sight.

san francisco

I laid down my love
but rue my first choice—
topiary edges, brittle colors
swept in brilliant piles.

I laid down in the praise
and the commentary on the praise
absorbed the season's somnolence
careless of its dense ceramic glaze.

Telephone wires cross dumbly
into bowers the incidental bird
accepts completely, a hedonist
forgetful of position in the troop.

Wise as it is to sit at dusk
and slowly process alcohol
worn trees pulse
and thrill to the tendril

At wind I too once walked in,
walked it to completion—
the marriage of damage and uplift,
chorus of scrape and release.

urdu made easy

I am fed up with this world
And want to be somewhere else
But it is no problem—I have ceased to believe
In disjunction, the trouble over choices
In a too-short life. I want to go
Outside the snow's dominion
In a cab with you in Urdu, singing
Through the beatific traffic, ruining
My housing for a song. Take from me
Split hearts with two desires—
They support me no longer
They're free now for you, you can use them
Use them to summon new blooms.

gulag

So sue me and my gulag—
the rope frayed when I swooped.
Not even approximately did I think
the load might hit one carmine riband
of your hair, but she'd been
in many bands, so knew the danger:
Truth saunters in so indolently
where you do not wish to go.

Now quietly you lie there
and won't stretch out your hand—
beyond any wishing, finished
with givens, Alp worn down
to loess. And while it's still gulag
you read as if to find a way to choose it
stopping the now in its prettiest nouns,
so many colored streamers loosed
in empty summer air.

Meantime, I'm this formal one
there at every column of her name
a crown returned to commons,
industry's crushed center for events.

Unsure where it's wanted, the poem
carries context that hints at country's history
of strife—a thin scum blooms
on the prison yard tank, though mountains
still reflect there, doubled
where they did not wish to go.
One splash unstills the mountains.
Double, ropes fray. Mine broke.

apology to pasternak

In back of spring, another winter waiting
A year where only groping proves there's light.
Boughs drop to the sleeping world,
Broken script on spoiled sheets of snow.

Suffering is not not being happy—
Lost stamps to the night's philatelist,
Wishes' places fixed in Prussian blue.
That beauty and its students now so bore me

Who'd praise instead the crockery
For breaking, who'd scale a wind
To sough in scraping yews.
The meadow's secret industry

Hoards flower, fuse, and charge—
Time's colored pieces robed
In names, failed kings
Who left the manors

To measures of their melting
Proclamations meted out in drips,
Forgetting glazing, April's shrinking,
Winter's riches worn to ermine sleeves

In years the hands brought
Harvests in from starving,
Year workers learned to wear
Their weeds like crowns.

**false consciousness is people not
understanding their actual role in society**

We knew they had more children in that other country
more hands for the fiefs, more lords,
knew wives broke clods in lines to glean the leavings
above the mud on planks with smeared culottes

And knew that while this happened,
while children shouted louder with the tapers burning lower,
the truths we made of suture and division
would measure out allotments for their grief

Exposed from the circumference
of the country we were leaving, emptying
the vitrines of our emblems of achievement
extracting muddy ingots and subinfeudating farms

Till the people who were naked
fixed the windows for the mercers
the most idle-looking people
were the first to start the hymns

At the temples that we built them
with their wives who did the gleaning, the songs
they had in common walking out in hardened fields
relinquishing the summer, summer's shame

At its abundance, the spit and sweat expended
just in lifting up the barns, a wreath across the lintels
bought of harvests and distinctions, a mass of wreaths
to gratify the manor's gross excess. Children,

Haul your wishes to the commons,
deplete the long demesne of future lords—
the sun, a weak sauterne, retains its district.
Will numbers, shame, or shouting bring it down?

the new world

Mercator,
    blue abider,
zones you rode
are dying, dry of wonder.

Sea expands
    muscled phosphor
sprawls, erodes
discovered orders.

Hopes survive
    the ends desired—
world map closed
in gilded psalters

Inaccurate plate
    of perfect azure:
blanks abodes,
evangels corners.

kenosis

For you who is Yahweh who is building
but you are building wrong

Eventually you notice winters getting longer
calendar boxes fill with soapflake snow

You are secondary and vanishing
a lord of clumped mascara,

Money strung as bunting.
All that's cold responds.

things unseen

Brief as the activities of man,
January's calendar loses all its places.
Do you look up and not want
to see it, a star arriving firmly
at the center of its cluster?

But length of days have taught us
to not need it, to only watch the calendar
go wrong. What else will get you looking
considering the shopping, tree's schema
in its mutable green sleeve?

Pretend it arrived, though no one
could see it, a column in a building
hid by walls. If you had believed it
for only five minutes
then you, too, have believed.

poem for bruce

Under the roof is the empty room
papered in requiem blue.

Partiers crowd the burned kitchen,
gold fixtures hook to cheap lath.

What is it they can tell you about absence,
how it abates, takes names

Becomes a wall with windows
faced on a formal garden, content

To accept the thin rain. The syllable
forgives the words that need it, a sentence

Badly written, epigraphs scrawled
thoughtlessly in books. Book where the hero

Confronts a dark riddle, book where
the suitors stand at the gate and are stumped.

What force brought them forward
stooping at the lintel, up the chipped steps

To the blue door in the unbuilt tower,
half-built, the new stone.

the new poetics

Snake, be quick—excuse of words
to make me sharp and want to write
waits in metaphor's sleepless taunt.
People, use stones! Compose things
slow to weed sounds boys invent
from drone's new lows. Saxifrage
in young stands lovers meet behind
nervous to dismiss significance
Ur-names meeting Ur-things
in the flowers, bees reconciling workers
to their combs. Quiet, writing
don't strike ideas I let be composed
but through that flow of breath that is not
my breath, split ore from rock
that's not my ore, my rock.

the work they do they do at night

They will come in great happiness
To our distributions of millet.
They will come to the millet and be glad.
Some are blackened, some stumble, some sing.
They lap at our wine jars, the ewers still warm
From their hands.

I know a hand
Whose stain crushed the wine
And bathing won't remove it—
The lancet, the lancet's begetter
Perv that turns in the bed of the lord he serves
A sweet balm broken, applied to skin
The doctor, the doctor's assistant
New louts burning holes in the stays.

I see plutes return from the bad world every day
Shut fields to plebes and feed them.
They shouldn't bother—we pass here for others
Who turn in their sleep on the heather
After burning night's theater,
The theater's owners. Who owns you
Purveyors of chaos? Who owns the chorus
That brings you your tunes? We don't
Know their names in any of the harbors.
What keeps them making our boats?

a field in england

call waste a peace
division ground

resentment tune
a win a wrong

self a hole
swerve advance

dearth a gift
loss recompense

puissance flaw
sloth industry

selflessness
lascivious

paradise
an errancy

it might as well be spring

crocuses eat earthlight
    wait in a thin coat of fat

the entirety of love
  is a delaying

but it is also absorbing
to be made
and remade in her image

sit high on your dromedary
  come into your crown

mine was the site
you visited least
before the net slipped

but who cares now?

son oscuro

Force in wind
that gives to your face
that rosy appraisal—
    stones surround,
but you are calm and magical.

The mirror speaks violently to you
in my song, but what does it matter
so long as it reaches your ear
    and beside you you want me
in the pallid quietness?

What I waste is my soul—
your mountains, your palms.
Salt in promised water,
taste how it poorly hides:
    no mystery,
nothing to ravel but me.

New paths for pawns
so universe in words can feel
what I feel: that you've made us
again something tragic,

Two nights in a country
where dreams are glad but clouded.
Despite the obscurity
   vested in words
I feel total now, the shadow
of all you'd wanted me to be.

after lunch, some poems

After lunch, some poems. Wild ember,
isn't it pleasant to sprawl on this grass
at my insistence, dropping the knife
for pushing the rice plugs into mud with,
eyes blue smears in summer,
two holidays from service?

No question's a dumb question:
Is it right for us to sit here and scratch
on the college's monuments
crude shapes over founders' names?
At noon the ardent moonbeams
all disbelieve in moon, recalcitrant master

At last gone to rest in the world
of crowns and kerchiefs, of colleges
persisting in the sun. The bride who made
your crying face will later make it better;

Set of curls, put down your labor,
the poem's subtle structure, grass
sustaining green. It's after lunch
in summer, summer doesn't need a hero.
The malady of heroes: to always be complete.

bug's psalm

The bug's psalm: don't get crushed.
Afterlives feel meaningless
but spring will come,
push out the nubs
the kids braid into pallets.
Take up your pallet
from lawns noon's hardly touched.
The small think gods
just loll on clouds.
Bugs think gods just crush.

he continually puts
autumn in his writing

I continually put autumn
In my writing, discovering
How I prefer your lineaments

To any thing this rotting
World adores. Scholars tussle
Over standards, elide them

In the sentence
I call to you from pauses
On sobriety's palanquin

I'm ready to climb down from
All that song saw fit to move in
Before your hum allotted

Spring's abandon, winter's
Measure, empty dishes
Scraped to wasting in a house

Of foreign sinks. Tell me now
Why I still come here
Preferring your appearance

To everything exciting
On a morning—digits
Stressed with message, zeros

Moved across a formal game.
Out of glare and surface
To make a wasteful palace

Lamps for burning up
The dying day, spent
On truant sovereigns

Slowly only breathing,
Breathing's service
Ended serving you.

tutor song

Where is it, the measure
　　to bring in most members?
The speaker done spitting
　　out more than his moods?

The bird who must sing it
　　best suffers song's purpose:

　　　　survive, reprise, get loved.

poem with line by kazimir malevich

I'll do that in part—
rebuild with dressed stones,
prepare for iteration like an administrator

Busy as fish by rivers swept
months when colors change on dates.
Send for the beams, I am building!

I ride in my car a great distance,
offer a jumble on a white plate.
Hours and weeks are continuously passing by.

The project's unfinished—
what use is whining?
They are roasting an ox. How fun!

East of the flats, a gate of regrets.
Short wheat, green wheat—
the deed anticipates its penalty.

Each form is a world. The work
is unfinished. Have you changed
that much? Have you changed?

mozambique

let us put aside intelligence
thinking is the plague of kings

let us abandon
the pentecostal wine of too much talking

feluccas easing into muddy rivers
flotillas on the high platonic blue

accruing all the pennants
from accidents of blueness

the months of summer turning
in their fiery chemise

pretending to be tired
of their place inside the genre

yet moving with rapidity
in arcs across the plot

which is still a form of thinking
a humming while you're planting

new crops to strip from hillsides
in springs that come too soon

parable

They have lived a long time, and laid a white veil
Over many girls. Puritans paint proverbs
Onto busy civic walls, but already they have joined the parade
To the sepulchre, big with delight
About being begotten, while others are left
To run autumn, strip fronds from borrowed palms.

Doubtless you prefer the ancient epics
To parables involving lepers, sheep—much lost
In the different recensions, but a message held steady
Through each iteration: Who is man, who
Is nothing, to command, accuse
For he loses in sleep his whole inner life.

sort of a north country song

took to the light like
light, pondwinter
sun on bream
       all gormless

so to all gormless
 things attend

night's dim
cadaver cleft
by rail

     gravid ewes
    in sordid weather

      gilded heather

anniversary

Sun suspends its wasteful business.
Flies plod furred braille of the sill.

I arrived here befuddled, days when
a smile became your completist ministry.

Feudatories scuttle, preferring to palace
a chance to lay warm with the hounds.

Spent leaves lend stripped boughs
to bitter purpose. Your way was better:

Space in the grass to keep hollow,
shoots bent to shapes on sloped ground.

theoria

Blood to babe to father's
laden table. Dance, said
the father, show us your grace.
Whose tattered cotton
whose weary gristle, heads
duly shriven, wrenched
in complaint? Cleft so a heart
works without wanting,
summoned to pleasure,
free to pick dates. Curve
into cursive, praxis to ashes.
What reveler considers
the number of plates?

the shape of russian literature

Kolya hung his gun above the lintel
and signaled to enter the hut. Pine beams
and a floor of strewn reeds, colored plates
slotted in a plain wood hutch. *"And what
if the dead rose up all at once, and how
would they fit in this world?"* The snow,
being finished with winter, contracted
to one loud brook, and I think outside
someone was dancing, beyond in the village
where we couldn't see. A rough wind
pushed the taiga—a drunkard pleading loudly
with his mule—and the sound of the meter that bore you
became the soul's anthem to hum and be lost in
its short commute, sky to steppe to hunger
to pegs for empty cups. Stars came up
quickly over the vetch, clear water
in a pitcher for you to admire, upset
as night backs calmly into its stall
dragging the wobbly platter of astronomy:
hunter with his gun discharged, stringing the necks
of dead grouse; cut rye stacked
in spangled ricks; still milk in common kitchens
let spill over basic earth
that turns, and ascends, and is endless.

**zoroastrianism is the least
well-known of the world's religions**

They are always away to places the dust escapes from
touched by the founder's words of things to come
and they want us there to meet them
we who left the district
working to deplete the house of purpose
purpose drained of comfort for a song.

a formal unfreezing

In order to signal the formal unfreezing
they've left us to drink from a brook.
And we're making no progress
eroding our problems—
life tings and is varied
as a new-poured set of bells.

Who will care when we're gone
and the offices canceled,
hours there revealed as so much air?

Absolutes go batshit when they hear this
but brook, bell, and bank,
ice and earth's ether: once
gods rage all this goes.

the new sobriety

Liver, recover.
Years pass and are salutary.
A thin scum coats
the ornamental pond
quickening spawn
out of nothing, working
a languid expanse. Life
is raw and indifferent
to refinement, as
happy using Leda
as the swan. Before
the whole system descends
into Lent, hush, bitter
organ, and wear your
brief colors—dim oranges,
dull pinks, bruise blues.

pastorale

The incandescent grist, plied sillion
cloudspill in bowl of glazed blue
teach me to be indecisive, like the given:
each minute a changed beach.

Form finds fame and ways
of being willing, going forward
collecting shiny things. Better
when simpler, in parity with animals
who do nothing to make themselves
interesting, while we grow bramble-minded,
thoughts stuck like fish in a weir.

The personal is boring and bestial:
when rain comes, I sleep under thatch.
Sun dims like a bulb that's changed position
where scholars repine and titter
waiting outside the repositories
with annals of what we surrendered
for something remembered together.

mazurka

May I just join Renee behind her blinkers—
moonlight's not for everyone's career. People
   think they need a life to nourish
the presences they want to place around them
but find the things they hold preserve a nothing
   a nothing that's the rule in other lives.

But if the future offered greater breathing
I, too, would join Monique and try to sign.
   I find it so amazing
that work is too constricting
for poets to be read with full attention,
   attention in the love from other minds.

I break from lurking only to be Sarah
her sheets and dues and days and business skills
   to say how much I'd like for a companion
to get my work considered year by year.
I suffer from an illness
that is eating at my talent
   a talent that can write when pills allow

The years to bring another kind of living:
we merely love and need our poetry.
    I hope the others don't look too bathetic
but this one really resonates for me
for me who is the person
who is trying to be living
    living through this reaching out to you

But only in the way it transmits moonlight
that doesn't touch Renee or work or time,
    can't bring Monique who suffers
better futures with her lovers
or make us watch while Sarah
cups her hand around a pill
    another pill to work to do the blocking

Blocking is not living
writing is not living
    working for a living year by year
is what the others say I must get used to
who use the rules to push out others' lives
the ones who live their lives no way we're used to
    used to push the ones who do, who do.

simonides

Simonides, whose bitterness
yoked art to memory
   stayed unimpressed
with host and god alike. Suppose

the dropped crust had occurred
at your table, the tremor
   floored your rowdy
hall of praise. Loss

provokes economy:
sound to scale, word
to fee. Ghosts
   learn death
from threnody.

his concert experience

Another year with you refracted
Into the situation of each poem—
Forms mope, get old, grow empty
Petty question, petty question, numbers
Answers, blah.

Another year of festivals
And trinkets, security dislodging kids
From hills, of sound inside the poem's
Tidy grammar, cloves occupying air
In sickened blooms.

I still want to hold you outside
Of all measure, under blankets under
Frigid stars, where it can be simple
And you'd be reflected, free number
From the tenor of its promise—
Cycles, circles, breathing, meter, blah.

The fretted skies, the tents
For fretful workers, the epaulettes
Promoters like to wear, and you inside
The music, its meter, brass
And promise, I'm holding you
For free: sound's stop, form's end.

year of the monkey

Of the whistle of the kestrel
through the backyard air
when it's spring and so reason
to care is thin. Who will detain us
the flower king asks us
from clasping the cowries
that hang from his hem?

Officials in satin feed horses
in paddocks. I am worth
what an hourglass steals
from a beach. We are swelling
like leeches from winter's
last garden. We are bringing
important ends together.

in the backlands of the province

The bones each believe in the hollows of their sleeping.
Singing to them doesn't work to wake them,

It's sleep as shows up in the backlands of the province,
as it goes on in time and the scene develops tears. Why

Solder sick hearts to sick raindrops? Falling downward
together, loosed by the rage of undoing the world

To its poles. How is it our sails keep up with
our sorrows? We are told we are led,

Now tell us how water is all the same water
since dinosaurs trod the world's past. We last.

he gives himself this one reprieve

I gave myself this one reprieve:
to buy each text the syllabus requires
and burn them by the armful. Winged it
through postwar, winged it through pre-.
A column in a smoke of hot resentments,
a basement for the armory's scared guards.

I made myself accept the day's obeisance,
made blouses from the swatches close at hand.
Adored gandharvas, complaisantly spinning,
spin beyond my thinking or my theme.
The given chose to spread its awesome colors—
I took them like the candy from a hand.